DEDICATION

This book is dedicated to all you little lovebugs

February was the month of love, and the town of Blissville was buzzing with life.

Critters scurried in and out of the post office, picking up and dropping off packages and letters.

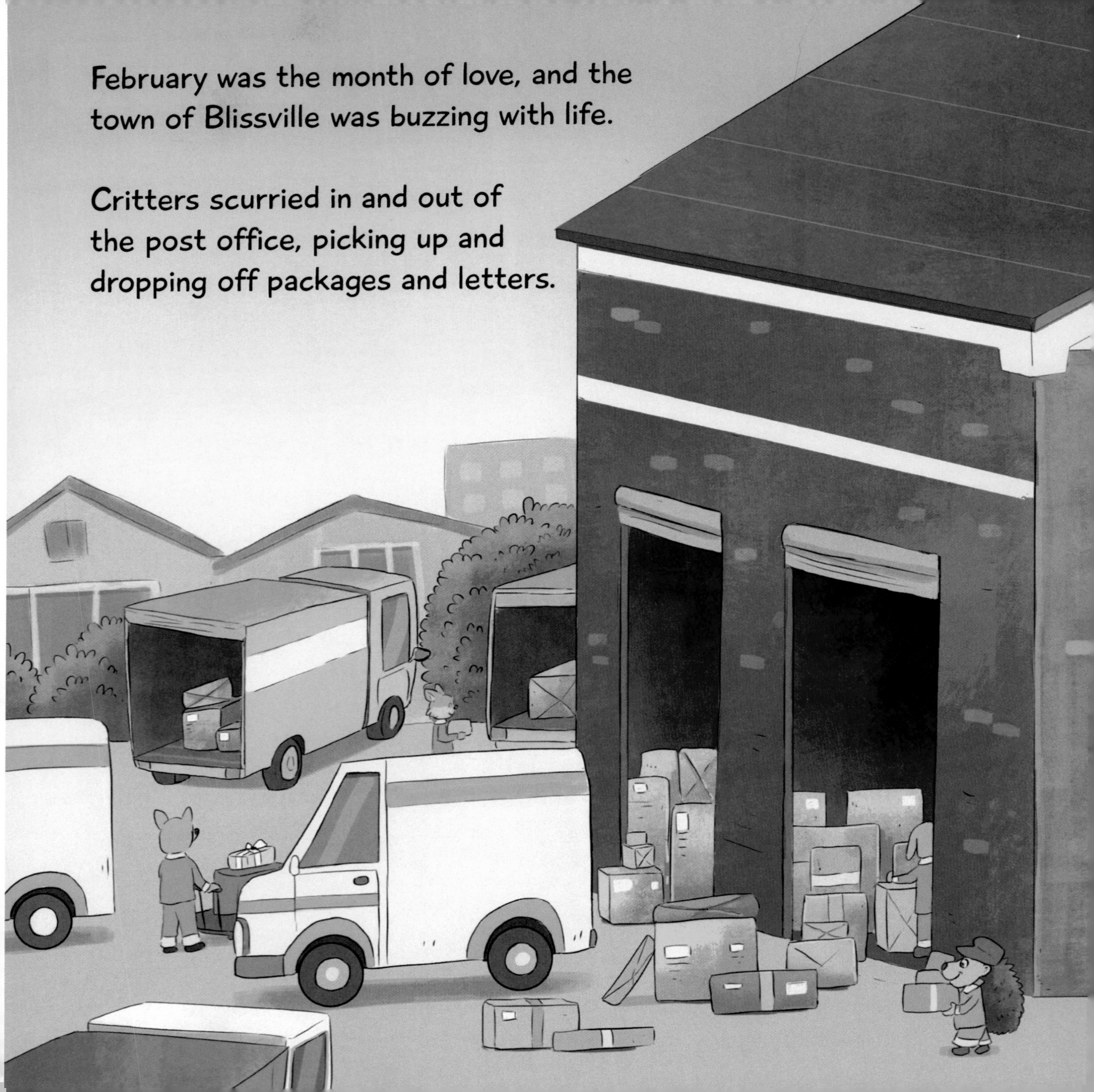

Loads of Love

Written by Sonica Ellis

Illustrated by Nejla Shojaie

ISBN: 978-1-7372647-6-7

Dear Readers,

Valentine's Day is a day when many people focus on those important to them. Gifts of chocolates, flowers, and simple acts of kindness abound. But there is no reason to restrict this to just Valentine's Day. In the words of George Elliston "How beautiful *any* day can be when kindness touches it!"

Until next time!

Love always,

Sonnie

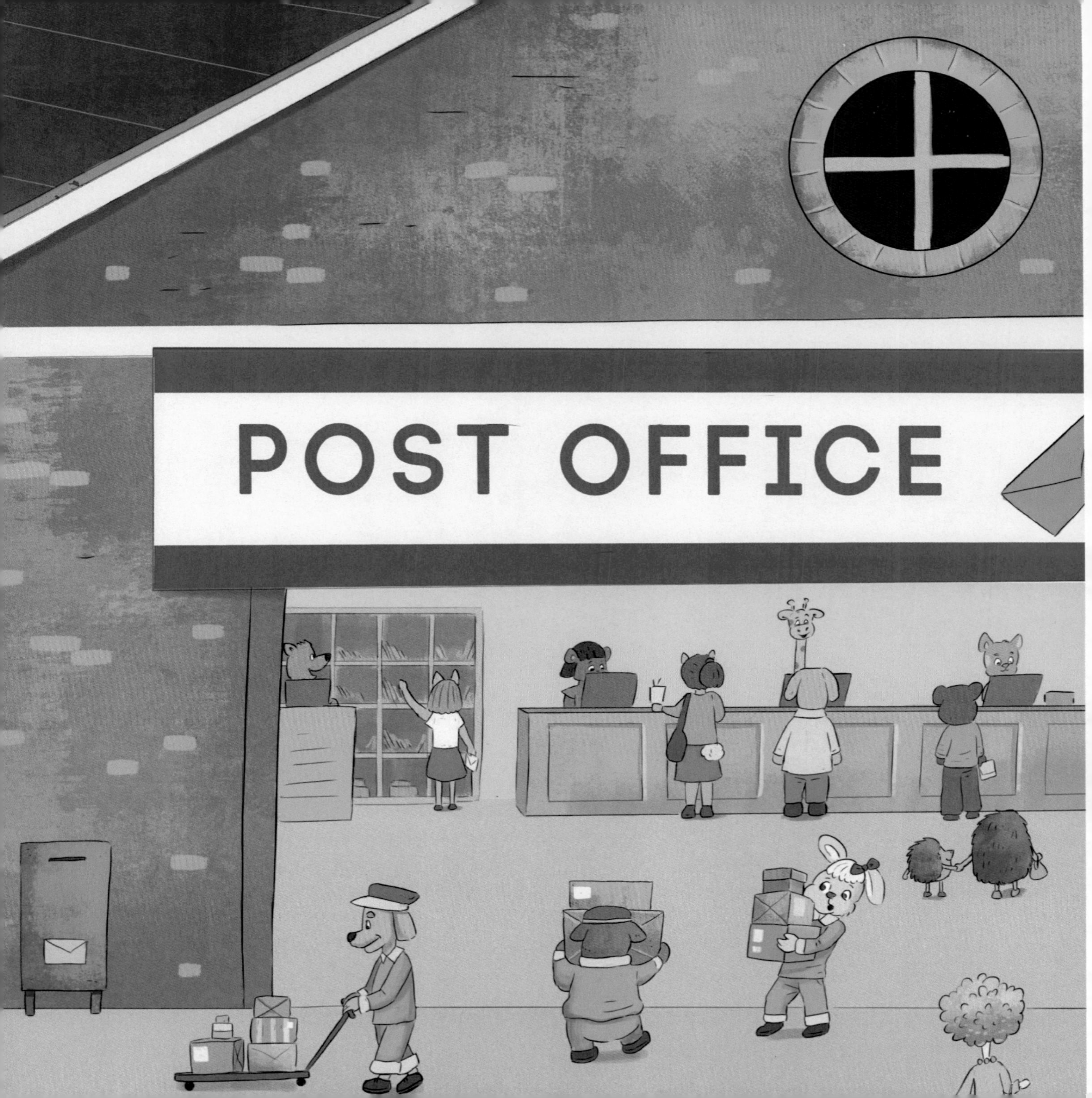
POST OFFICE

Larry the Mail Truck could be seen making several trips down the busy streets, loaded with neatly wrapped packages.

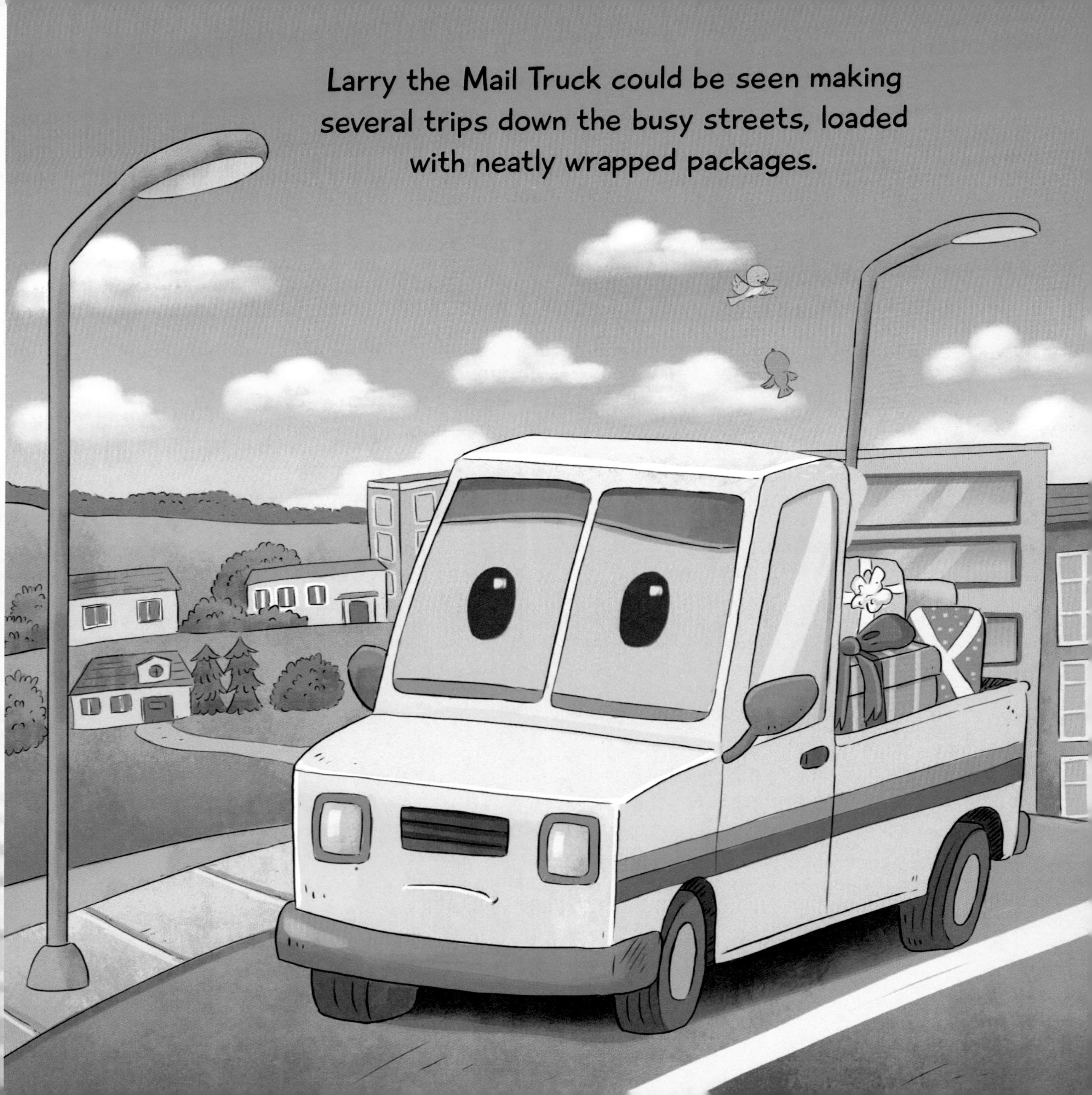

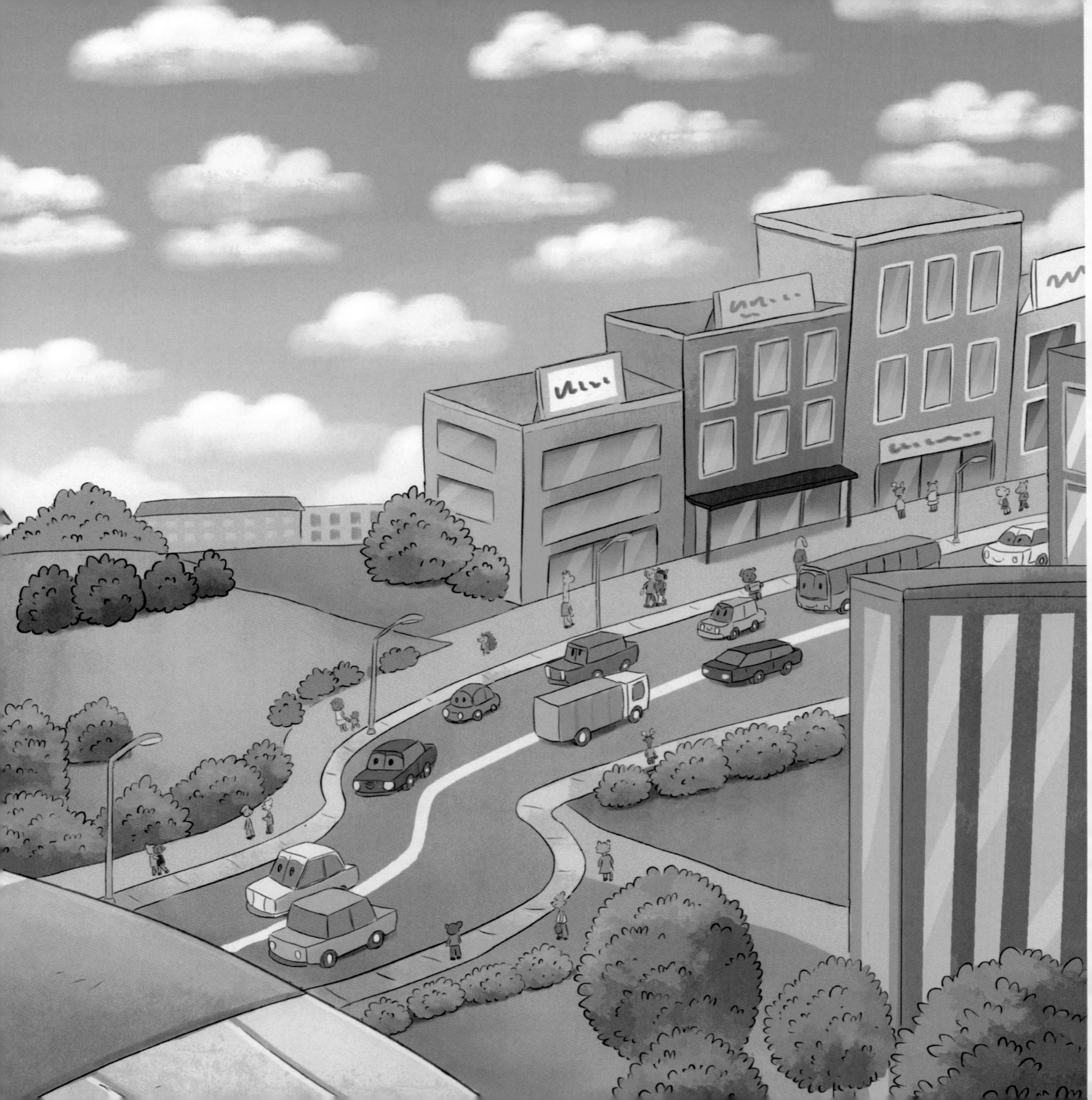

It was the day before Valentine's Day, and Bonnie the Truck was on her way to the Blissville craft store when she saw Larry resting under a nearby tree.

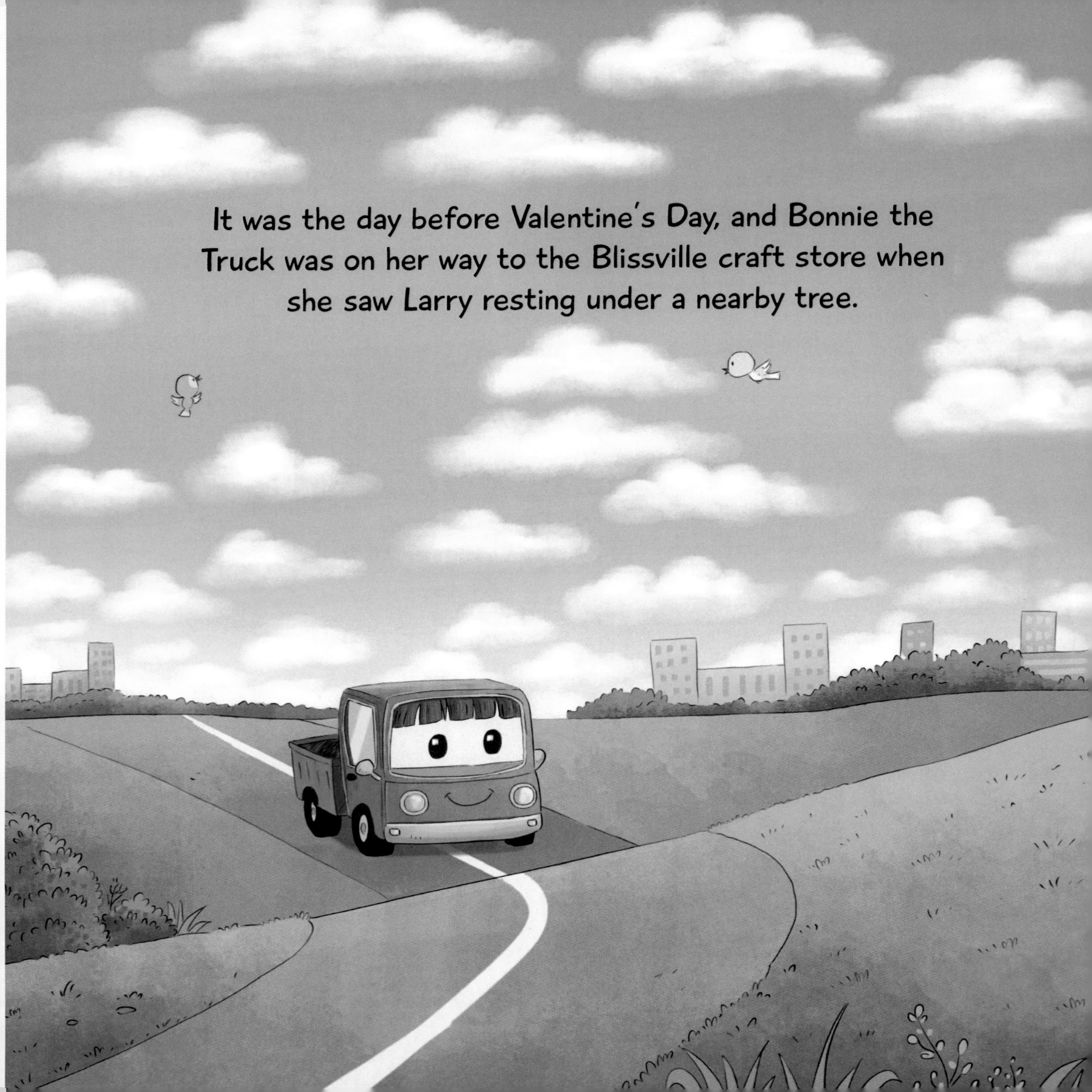

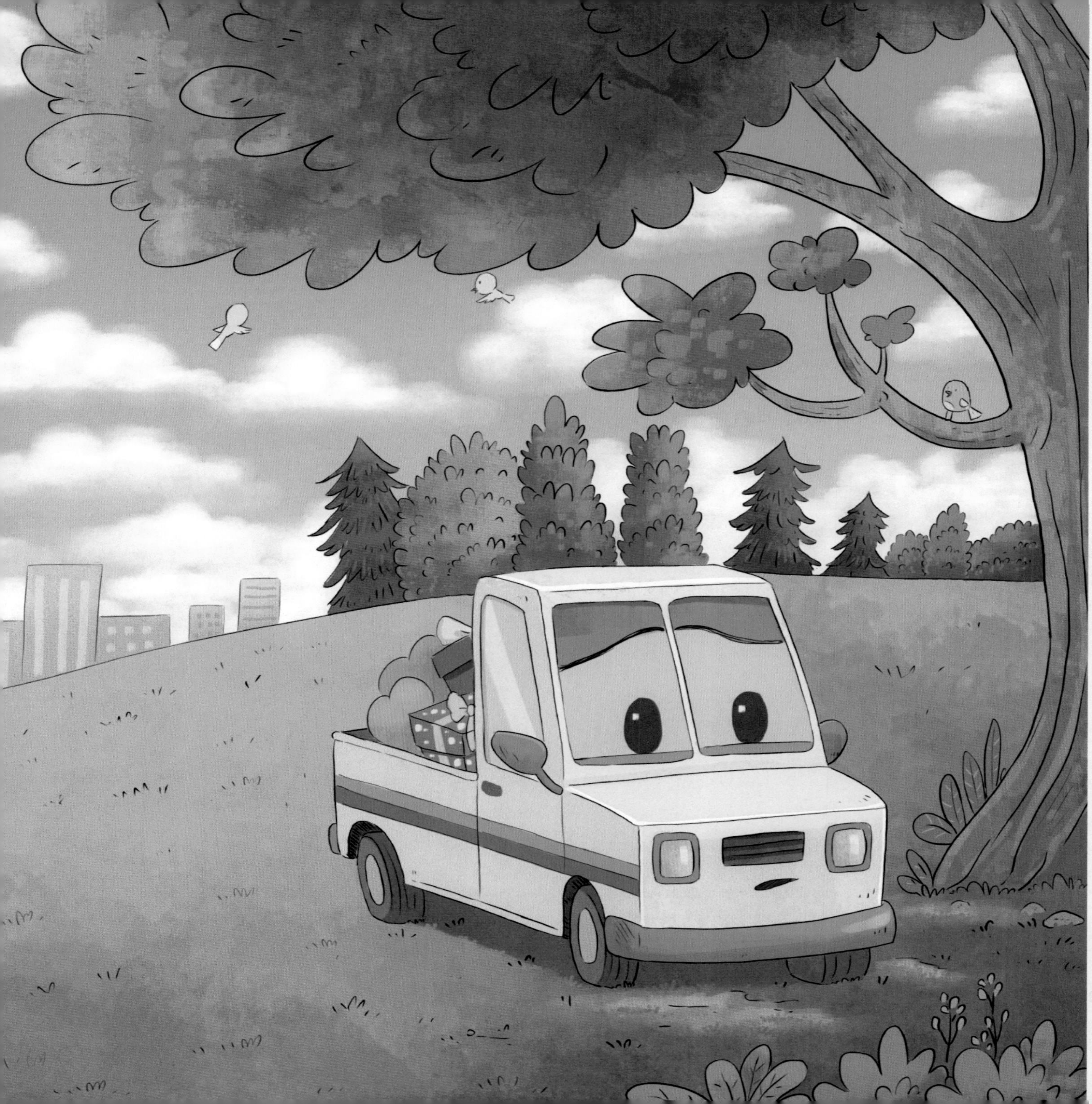

"Hello Larry, is everything all right?" asked Bonnie.
"Well Bonnie, "Larry began, but before he could finish he let out an enormous "ACHOOOOOOOOOOOO!"

"Oh, dear," Larry said sadly. "It seems that I have caught a cold. I'm afraid I won't be able to deliver all these presents today."

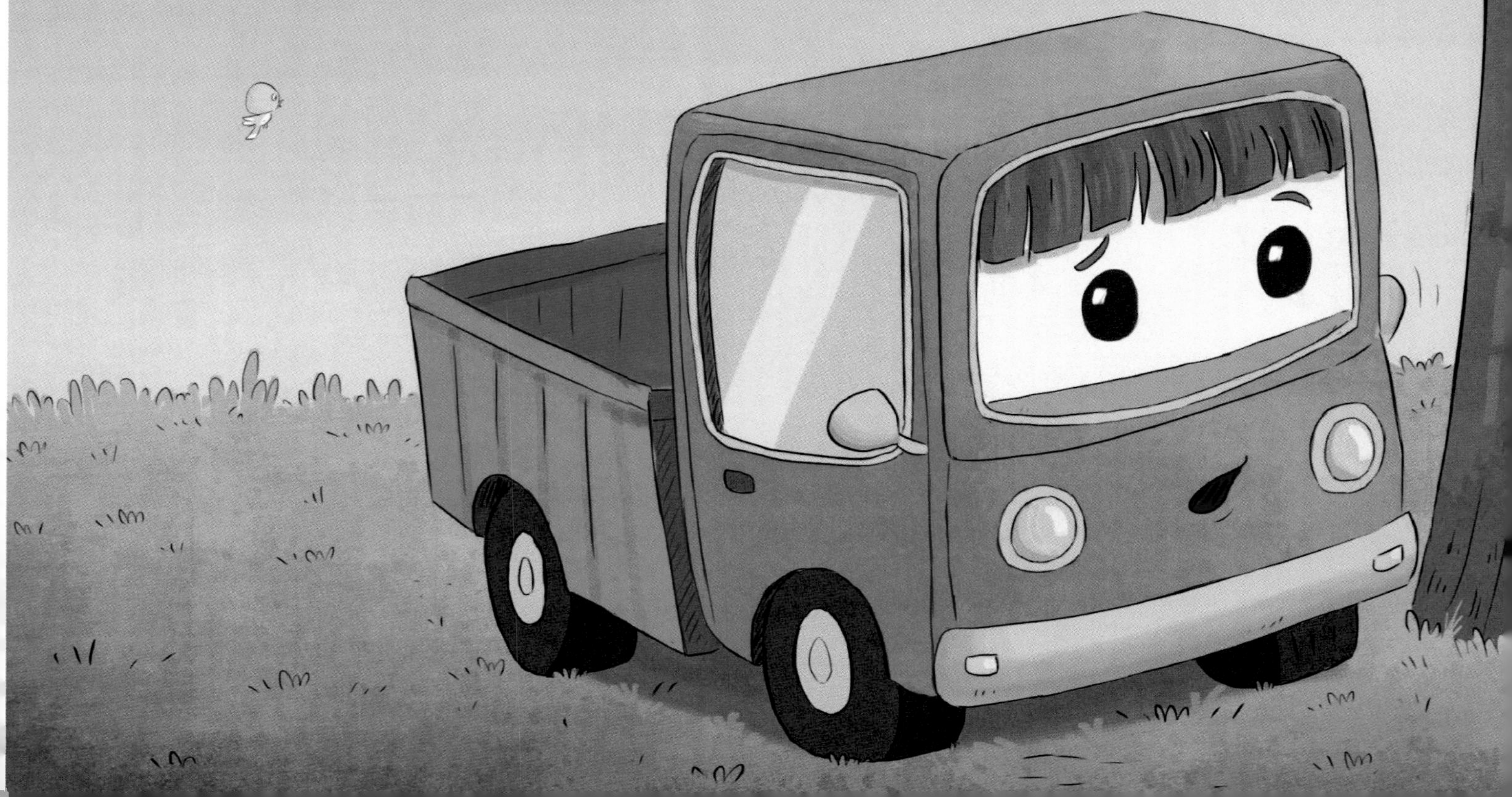

"I am truly sorry," he continued. "All the citizens of Blissville were depending on me. Now, they won't get their Valentine gifts!"

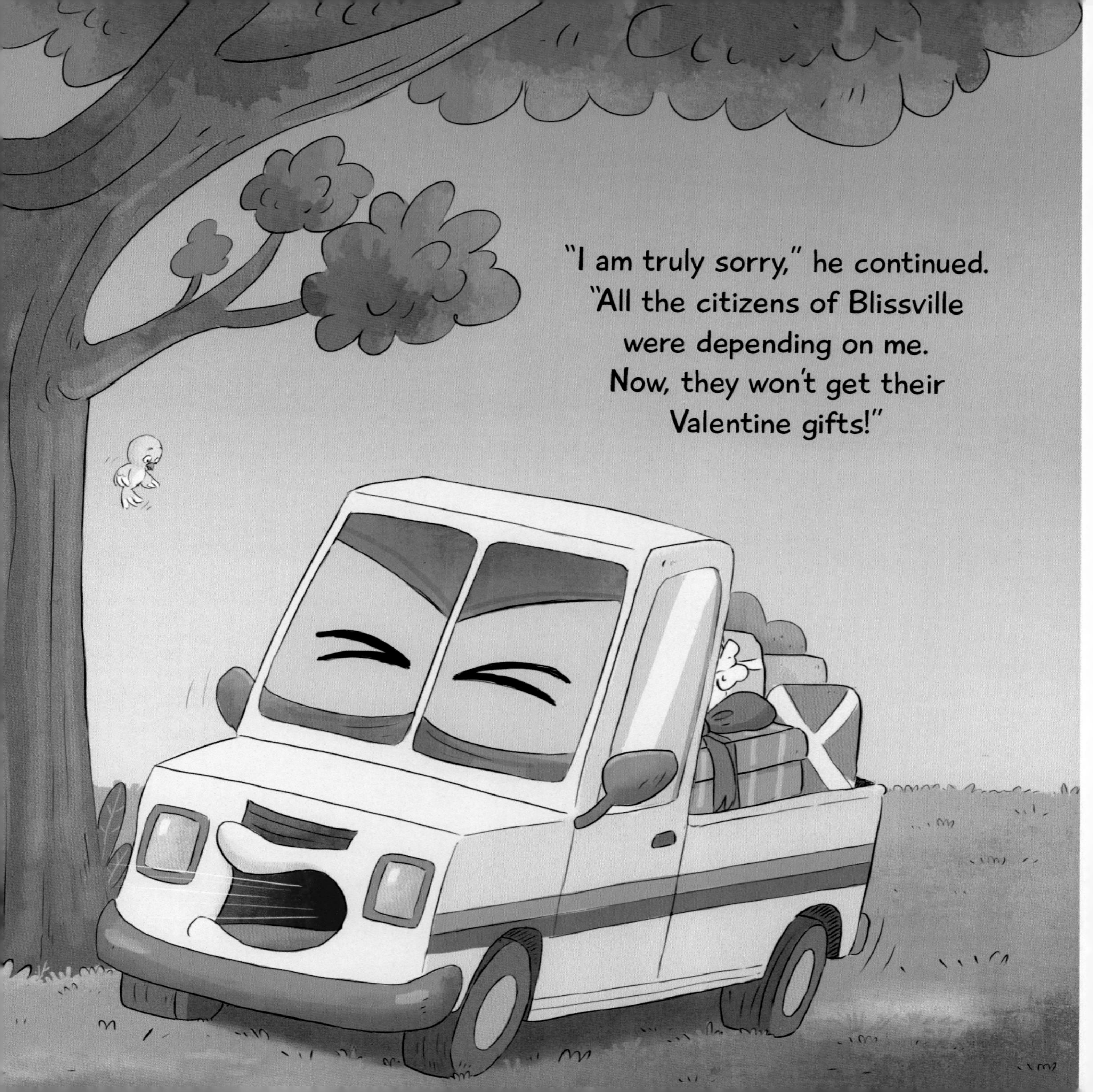

"It's not your fault," replied Bonnie. "You're sick. I'm sure they'll all understand. Your health comes first, Larry. I think you should go home and get some rest."

"I think you're right, Bonnie," said Larry.

Just as he turned to leave, Bonnie had an idea! "Larry, what if I deliver the presents for you?" she asked.

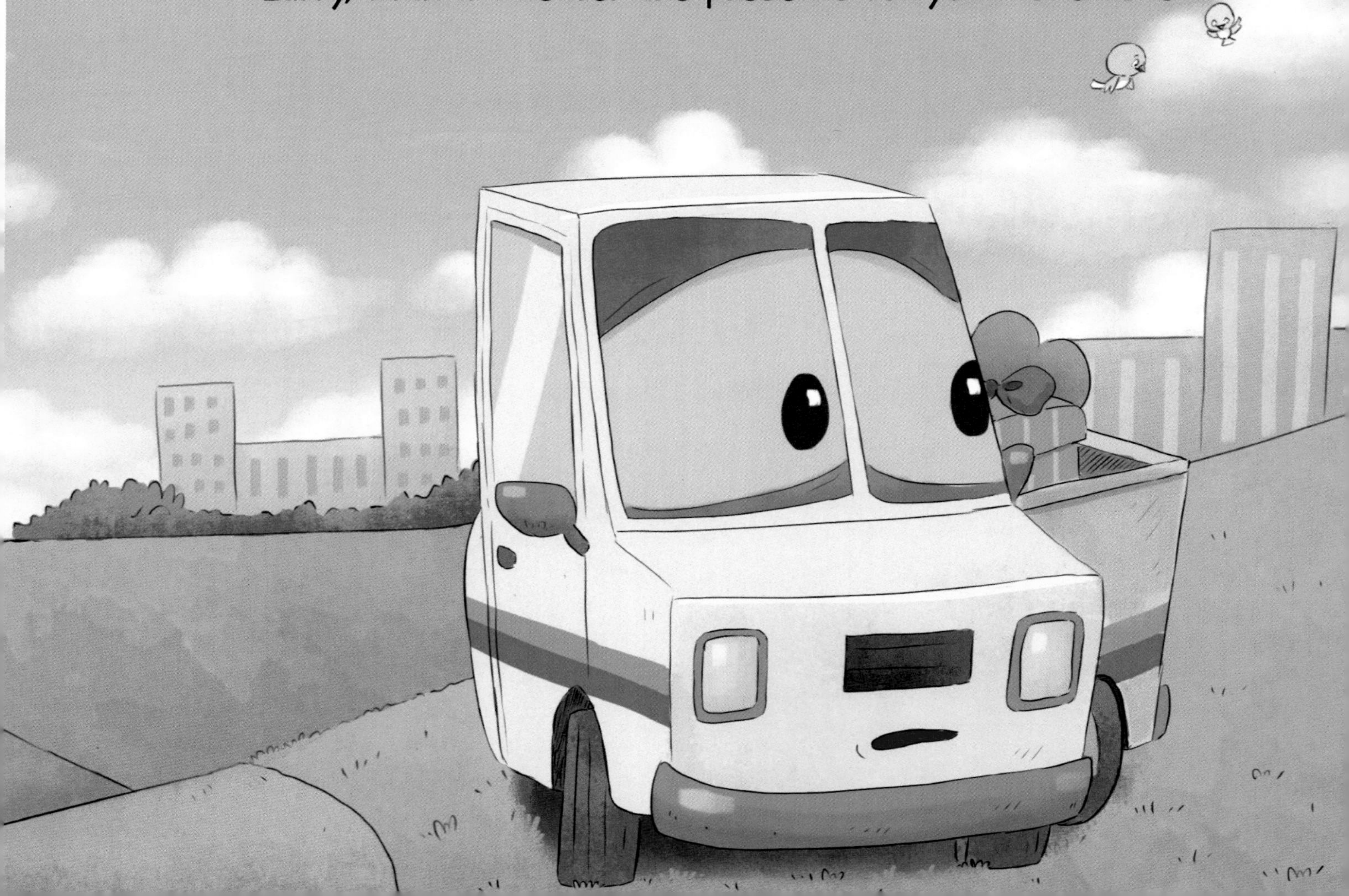

"Are you sure, Bonnie?" Larry said. "That would be greatly appreciated."

"Yes. I'm sure. Just tell me where to take them, and I'll drop them off for you."

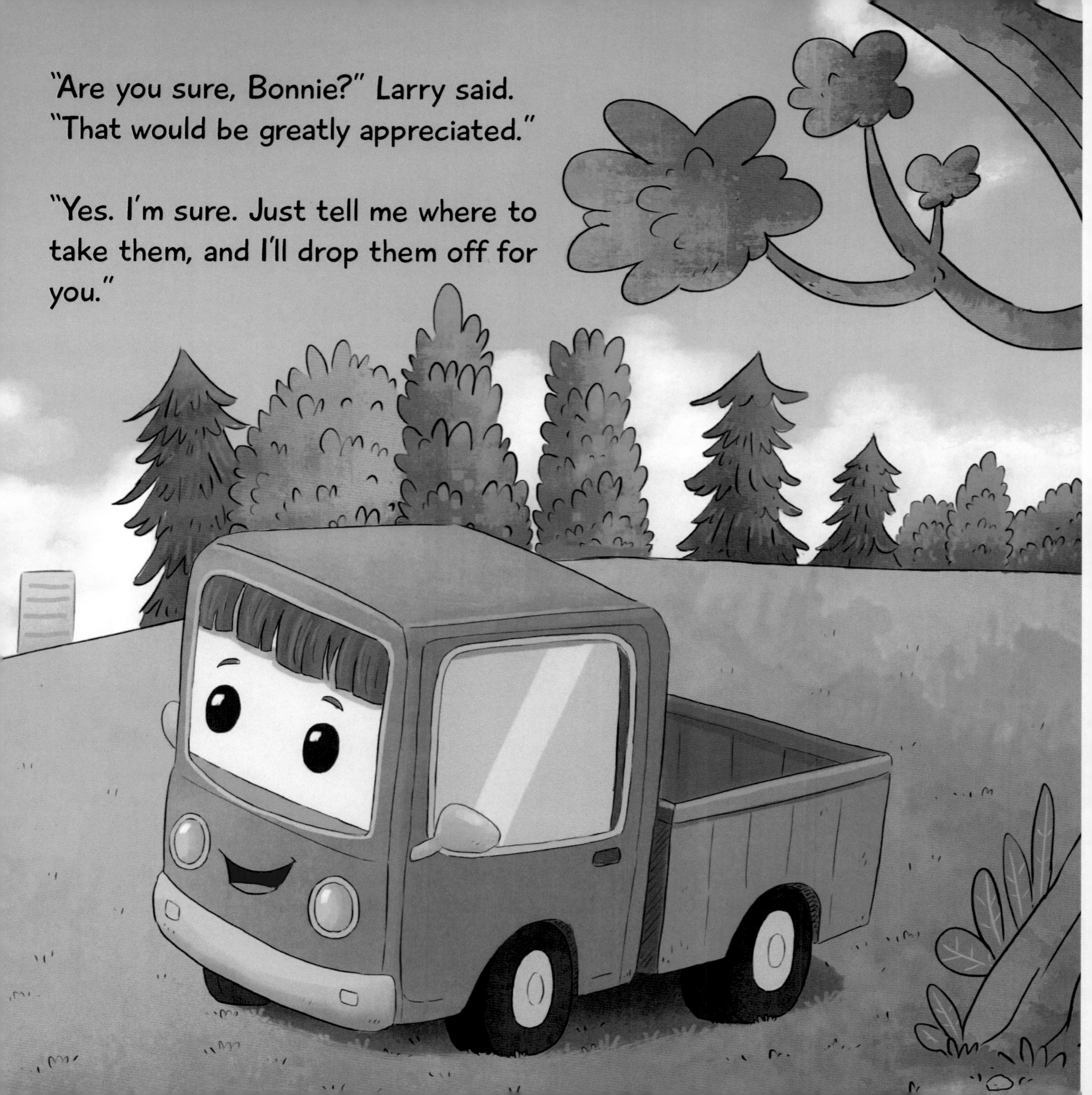

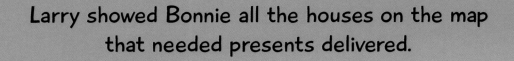

Larry showed Bonnie all the houses on the map
that needed presents delivered.

It wasn't long before Bonnie was on her way.

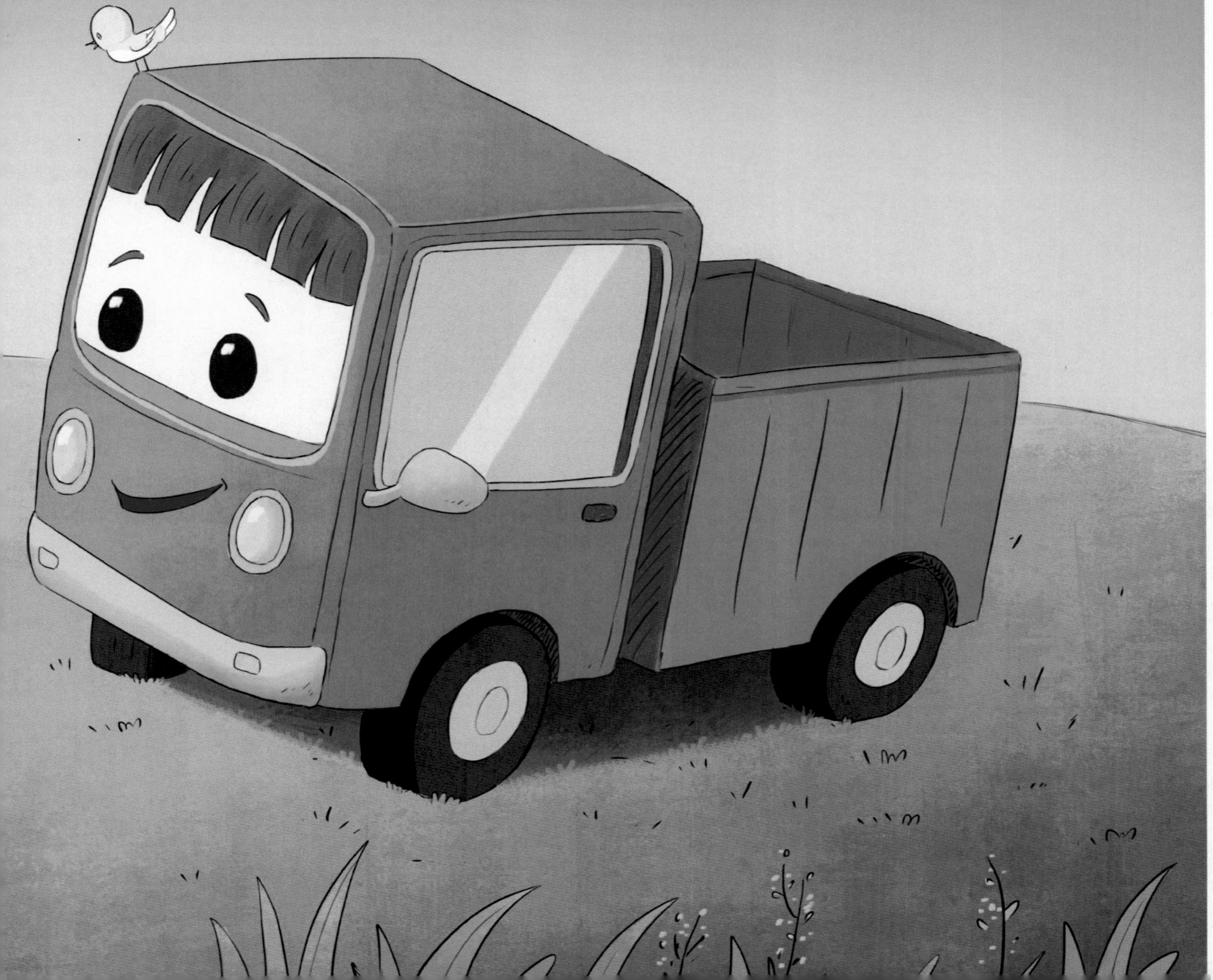

Her first stop was at Bill the Duck's house.

"Delivery!" Bonnie beeped.

Bill thanked Bonnie, and off she went to the next house.

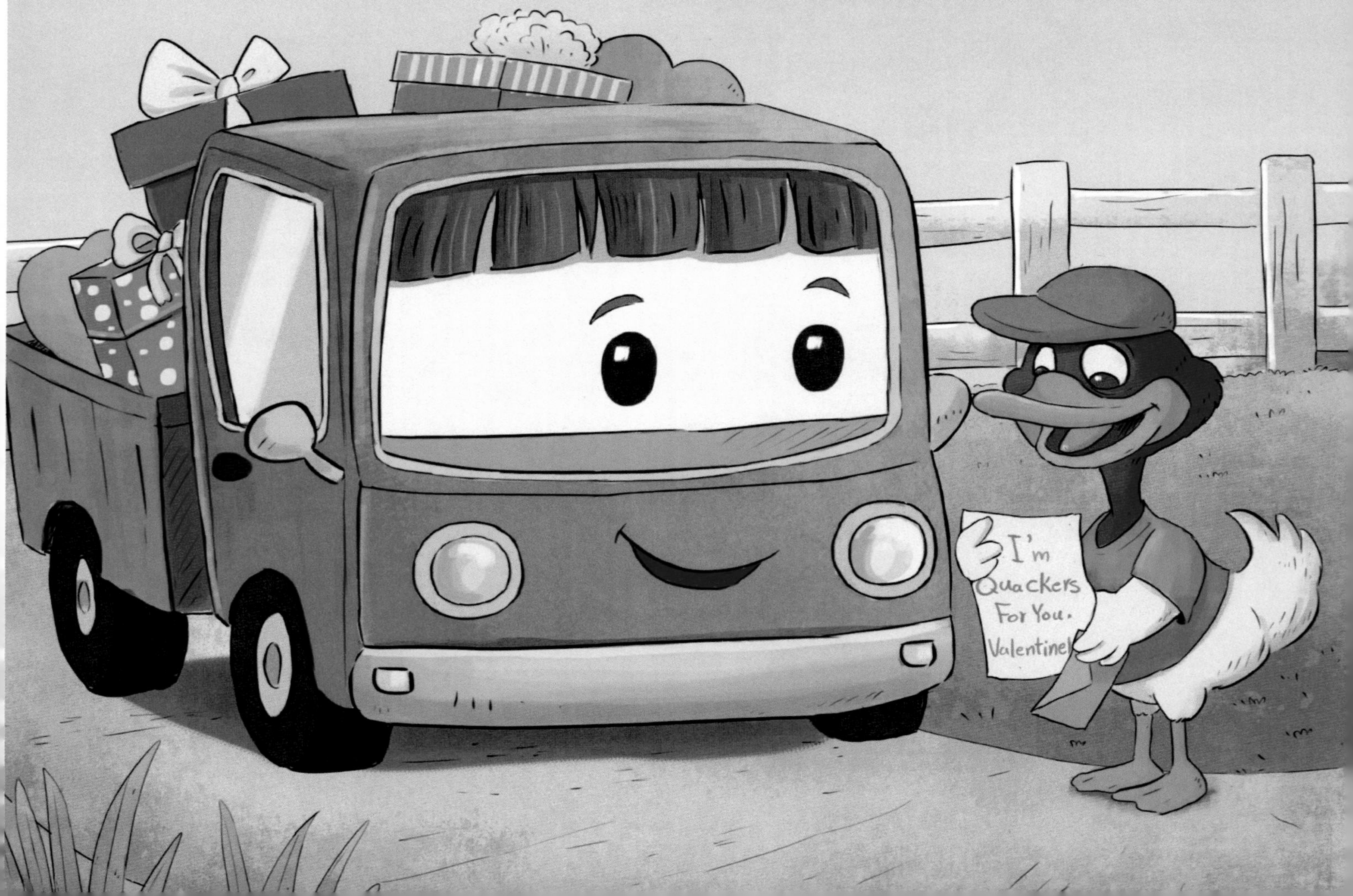
I'm
Quackers
For You.
Valentine

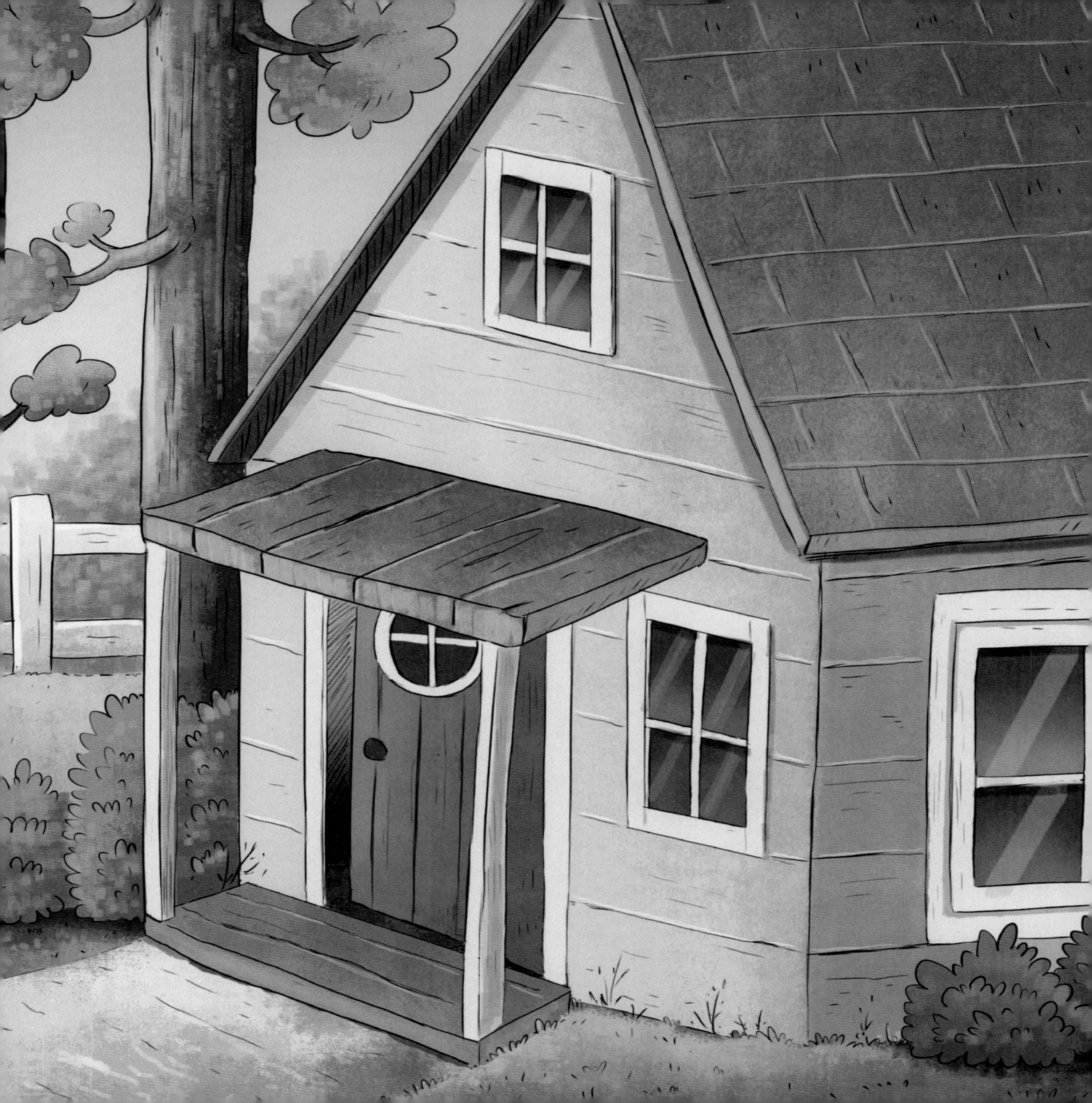

Soon, she arrived at Curly the Pig's house.

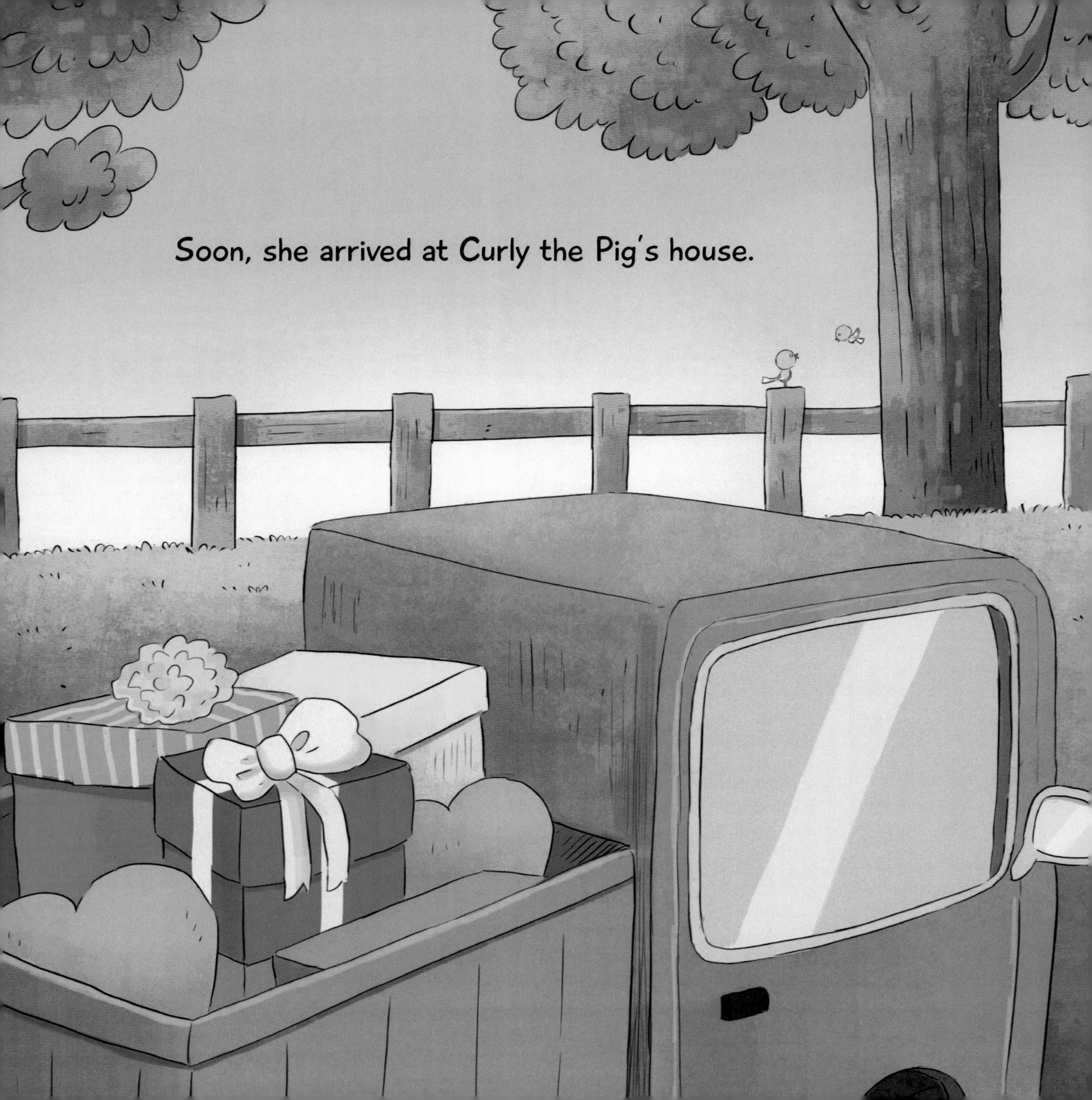

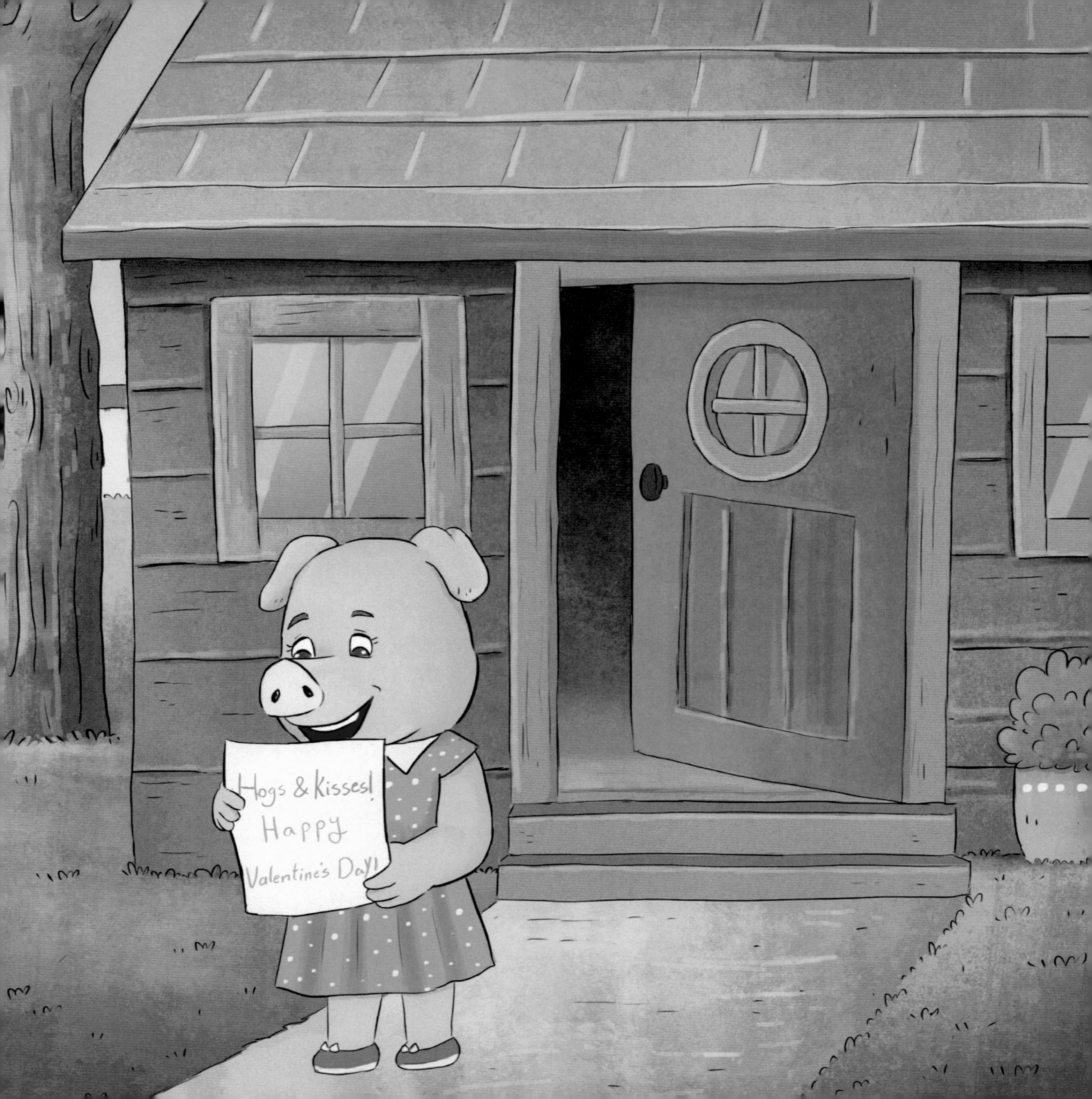
Hogs & Kisses!
Happy
Valentine's Day!

Next, she arrived at Daisy the Cow's house.

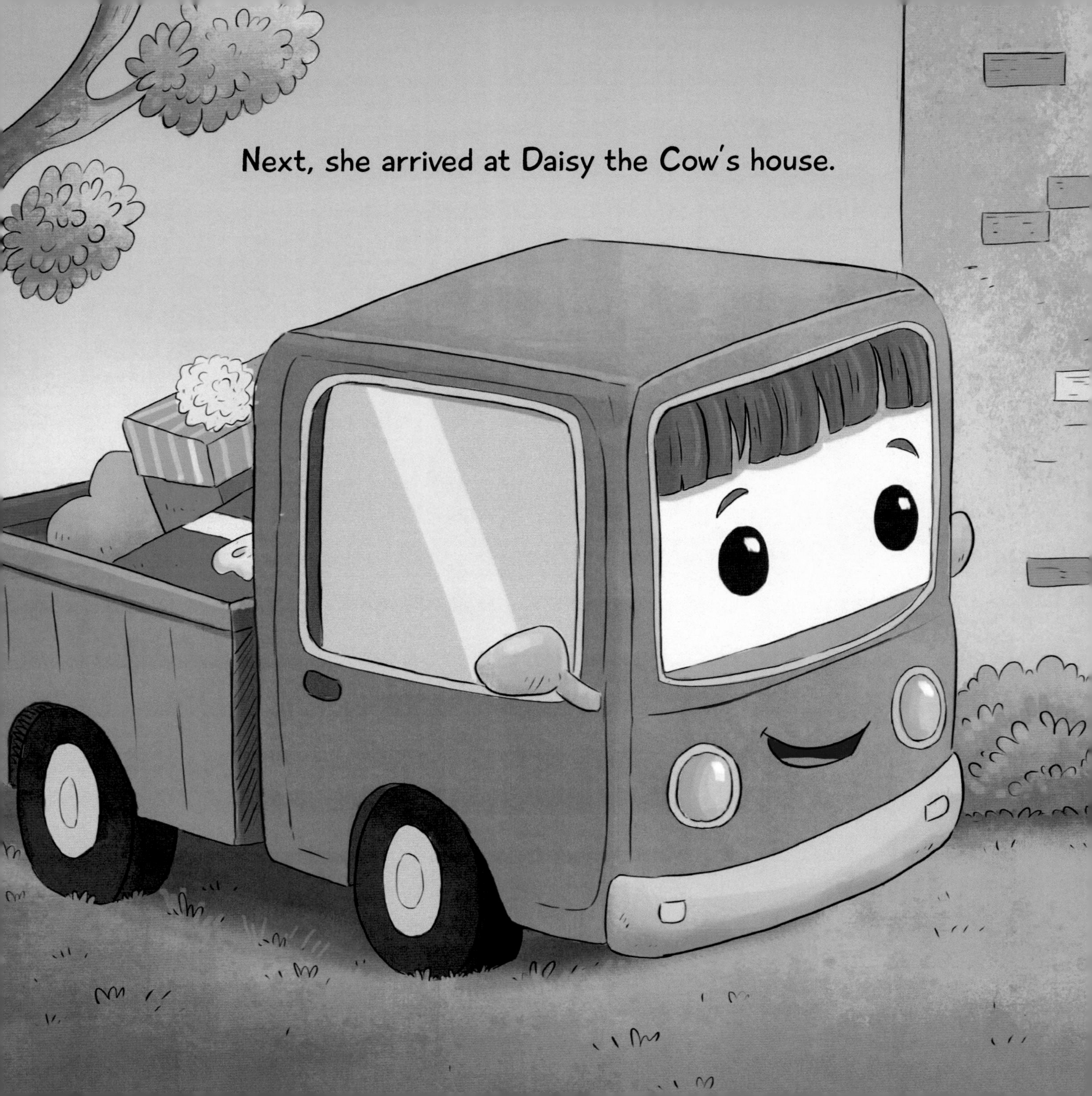

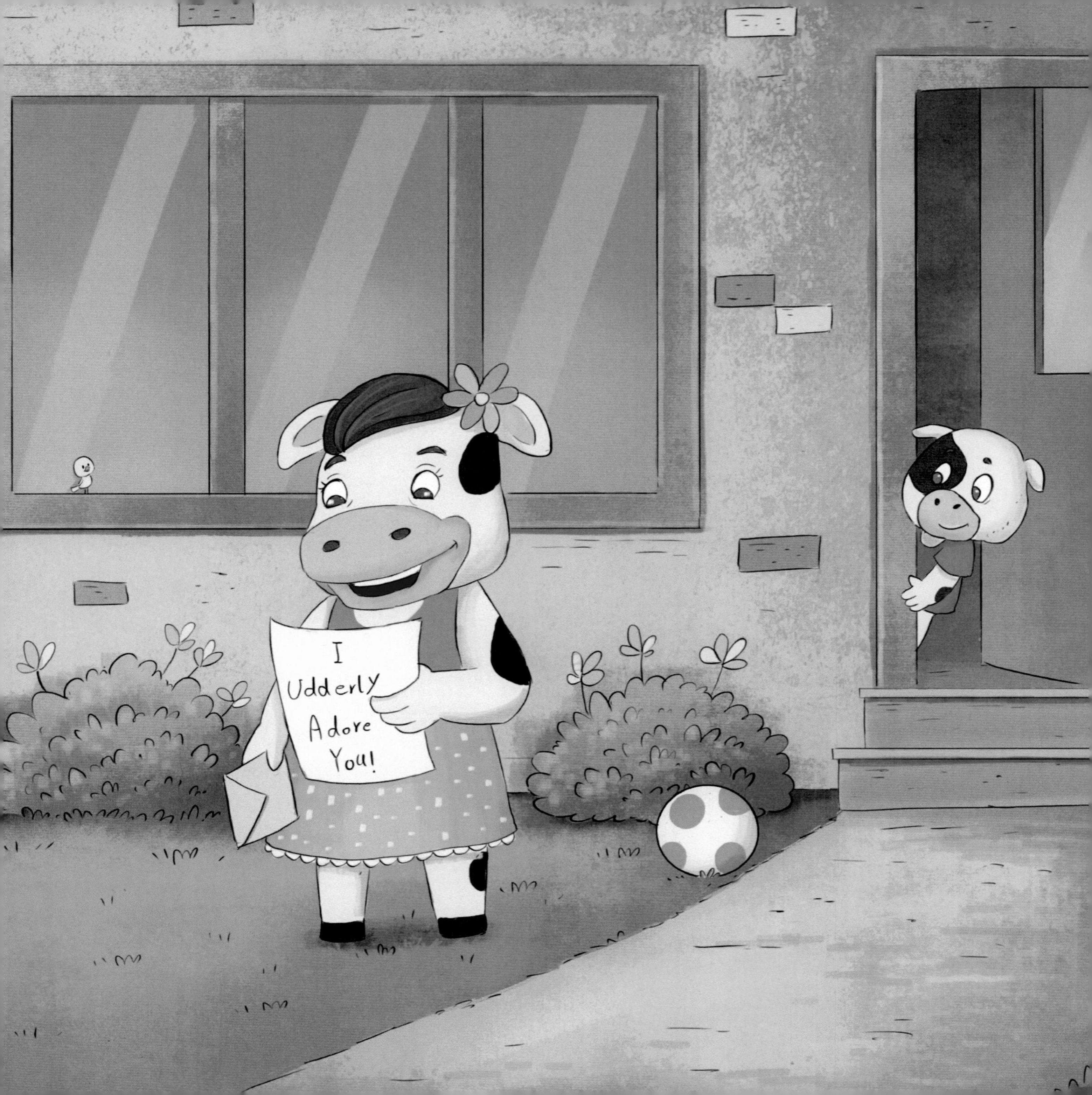
I Udderly Adore You!

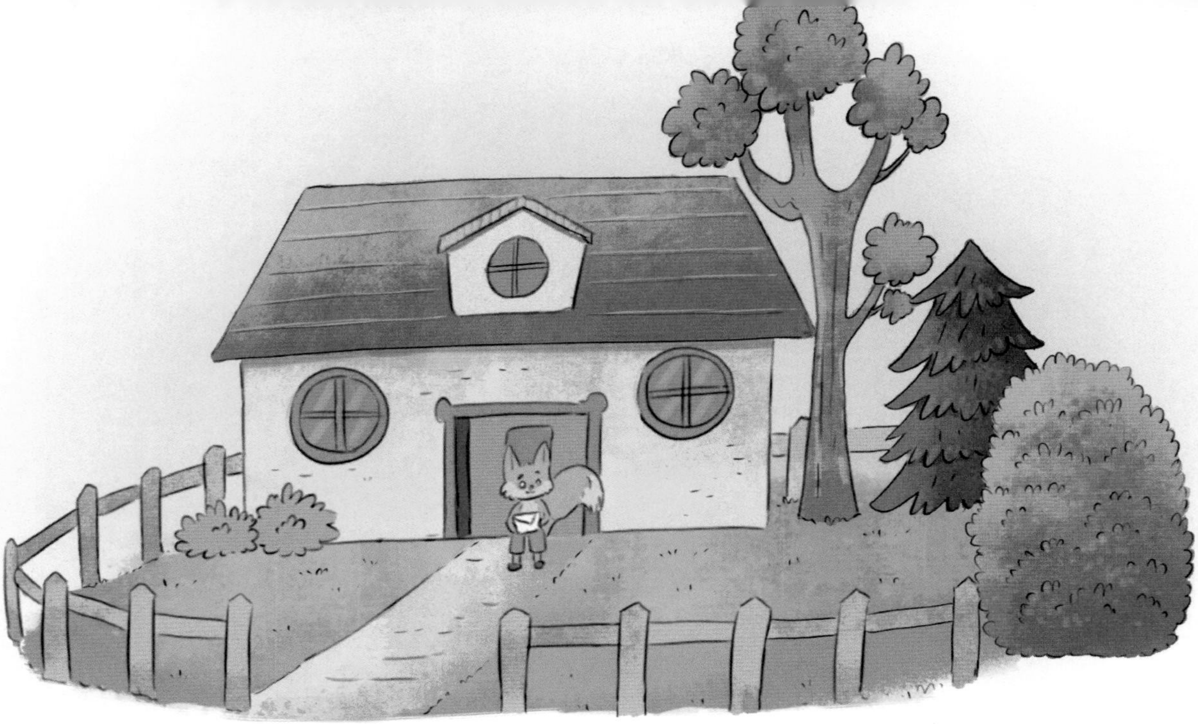

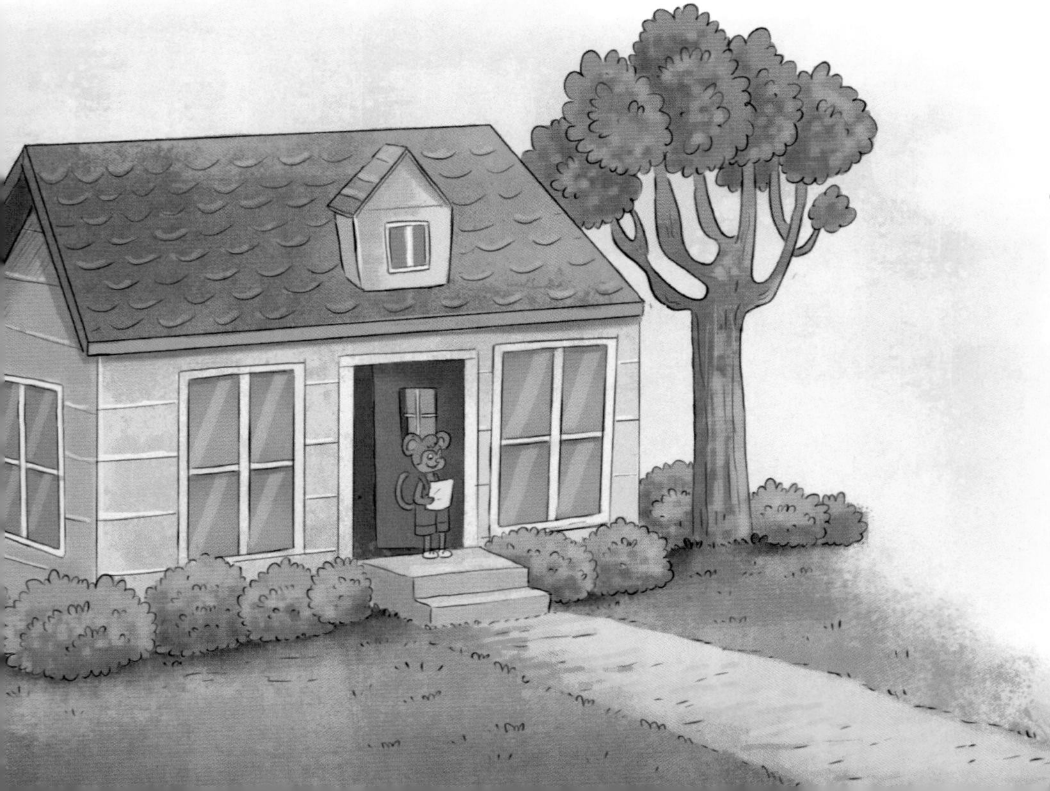

Then she stopped at
four more houses.

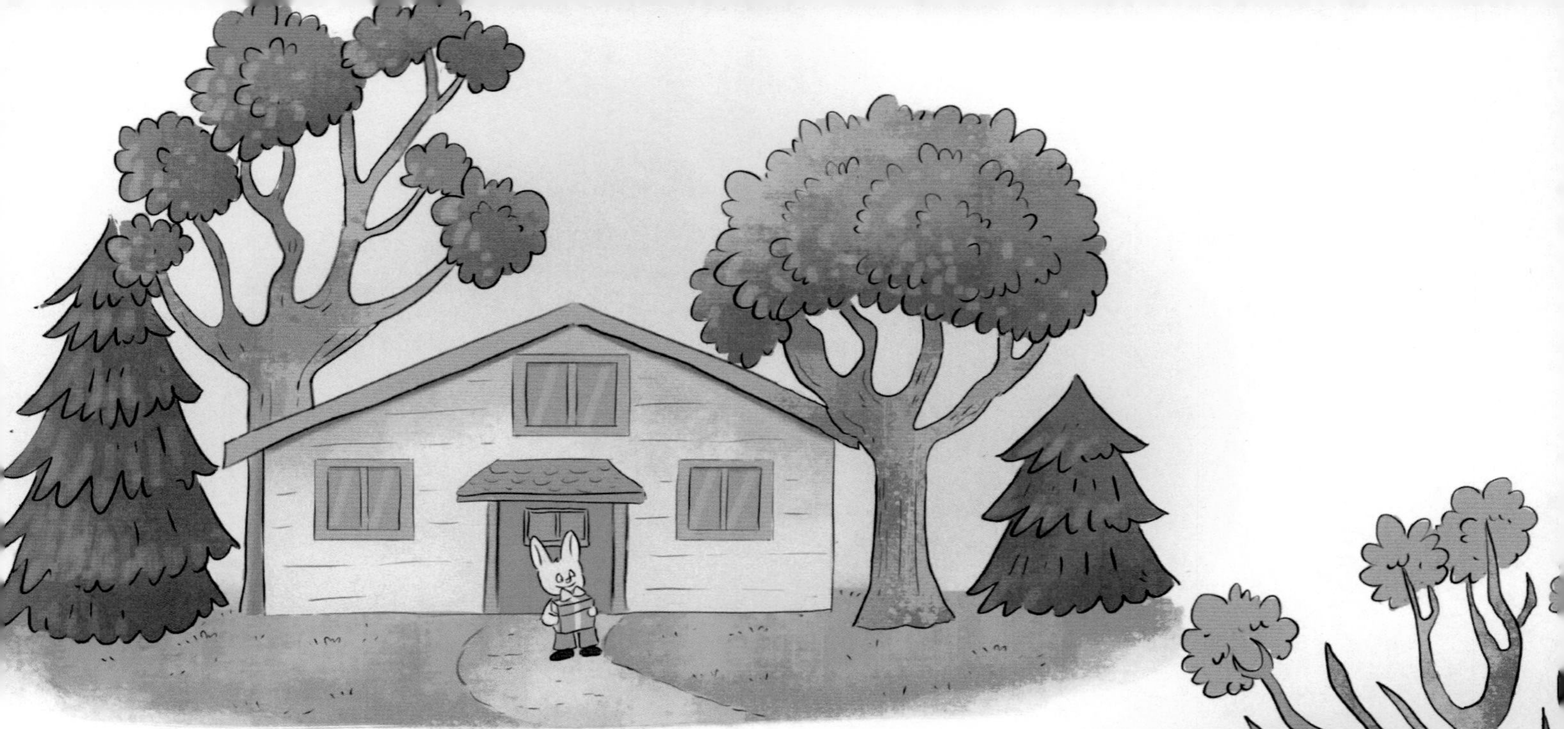

"Delivering presents is
harder than I thought,"
Bonnie said to herself.

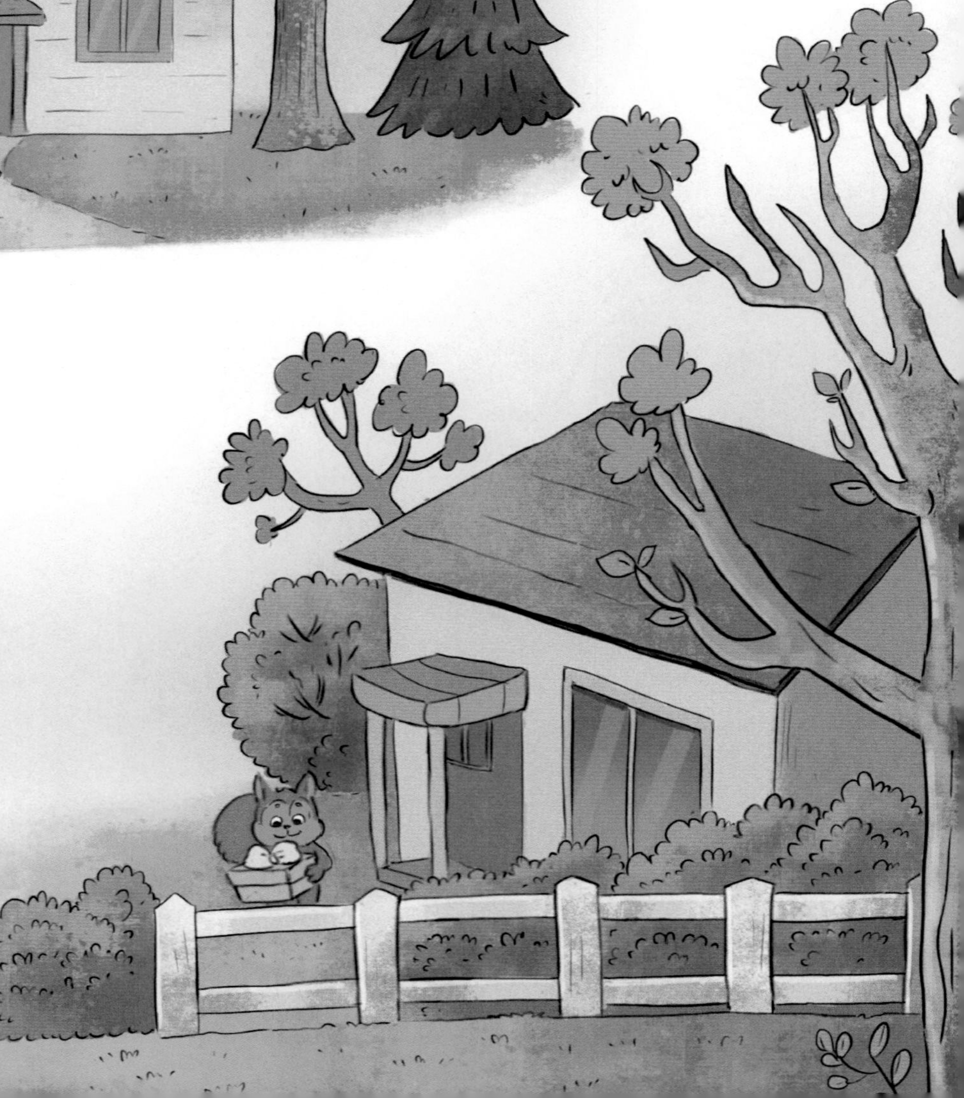

Finally, she stopped at Larry's house.
"Delivery! For Mr. and Mrs. Larry!" shouted Bonnie.

Mrs. Larry thanked Bonnie for helping
Larry by giving her a present of her own.
Bonnie thanked her, and off she went once more.

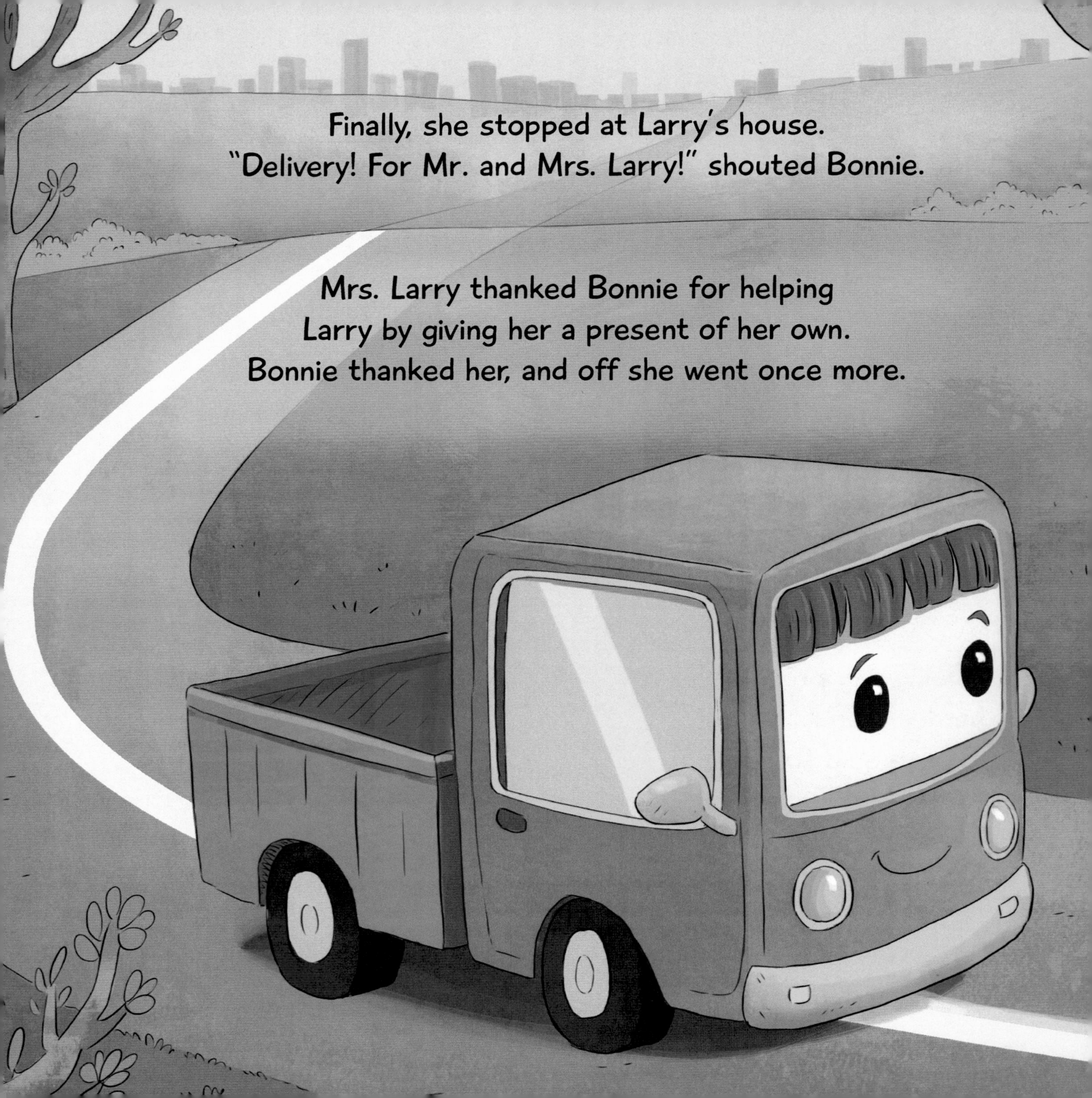

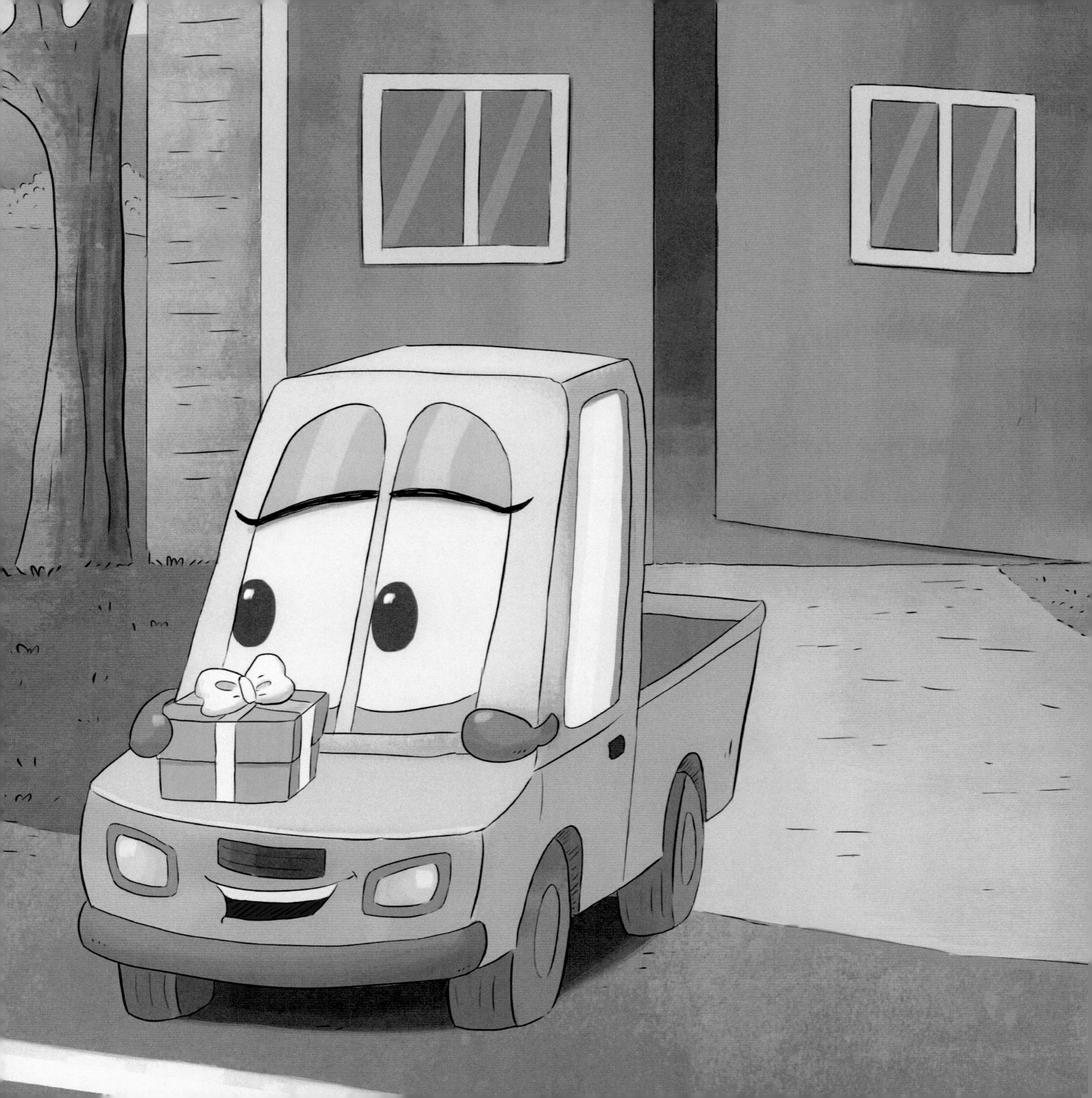

Everyone in Blissville was happy to receive their presents from their families and friends.

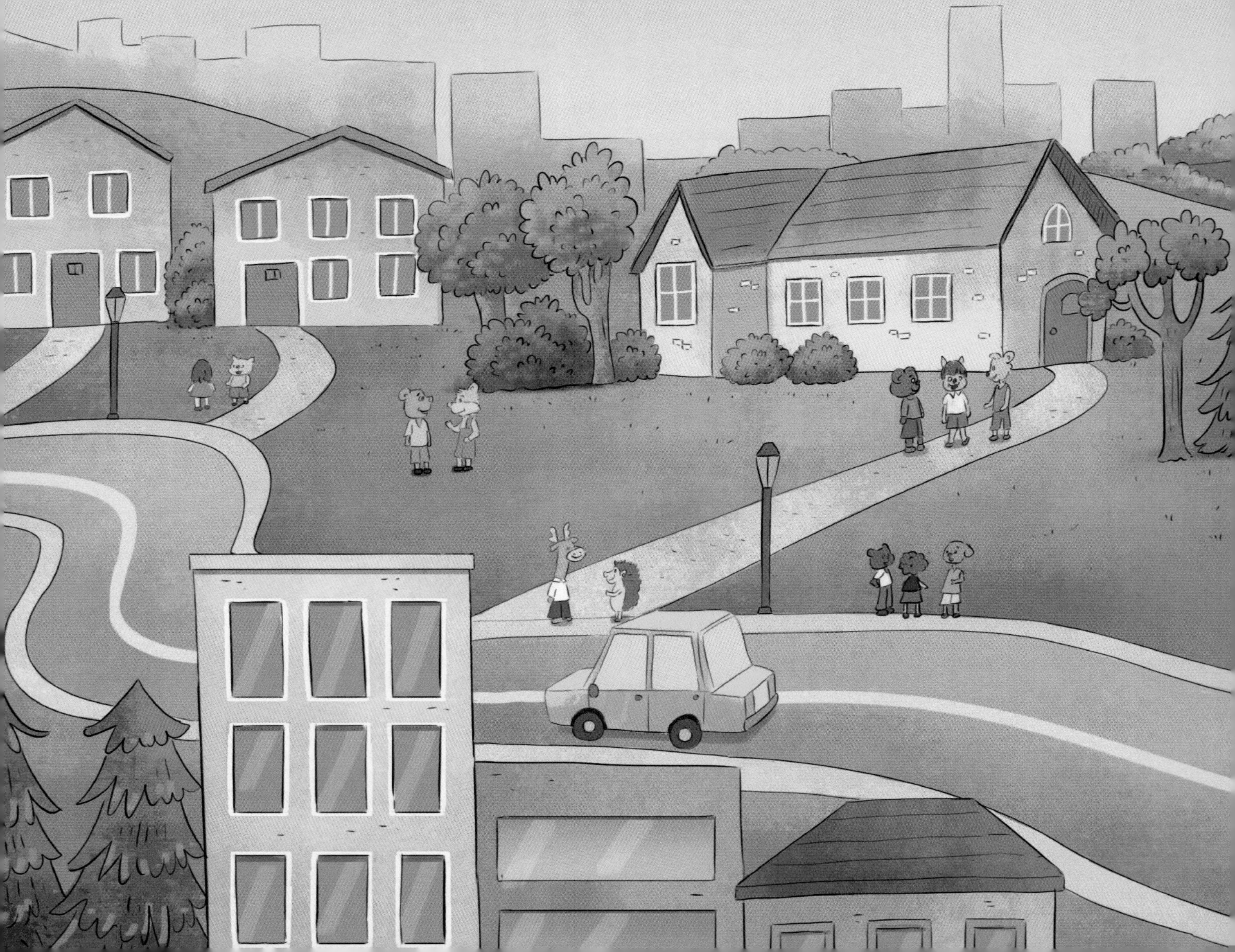

But Bonnie soon realized that she had forgotten to give someone important a Valentine's Day card.

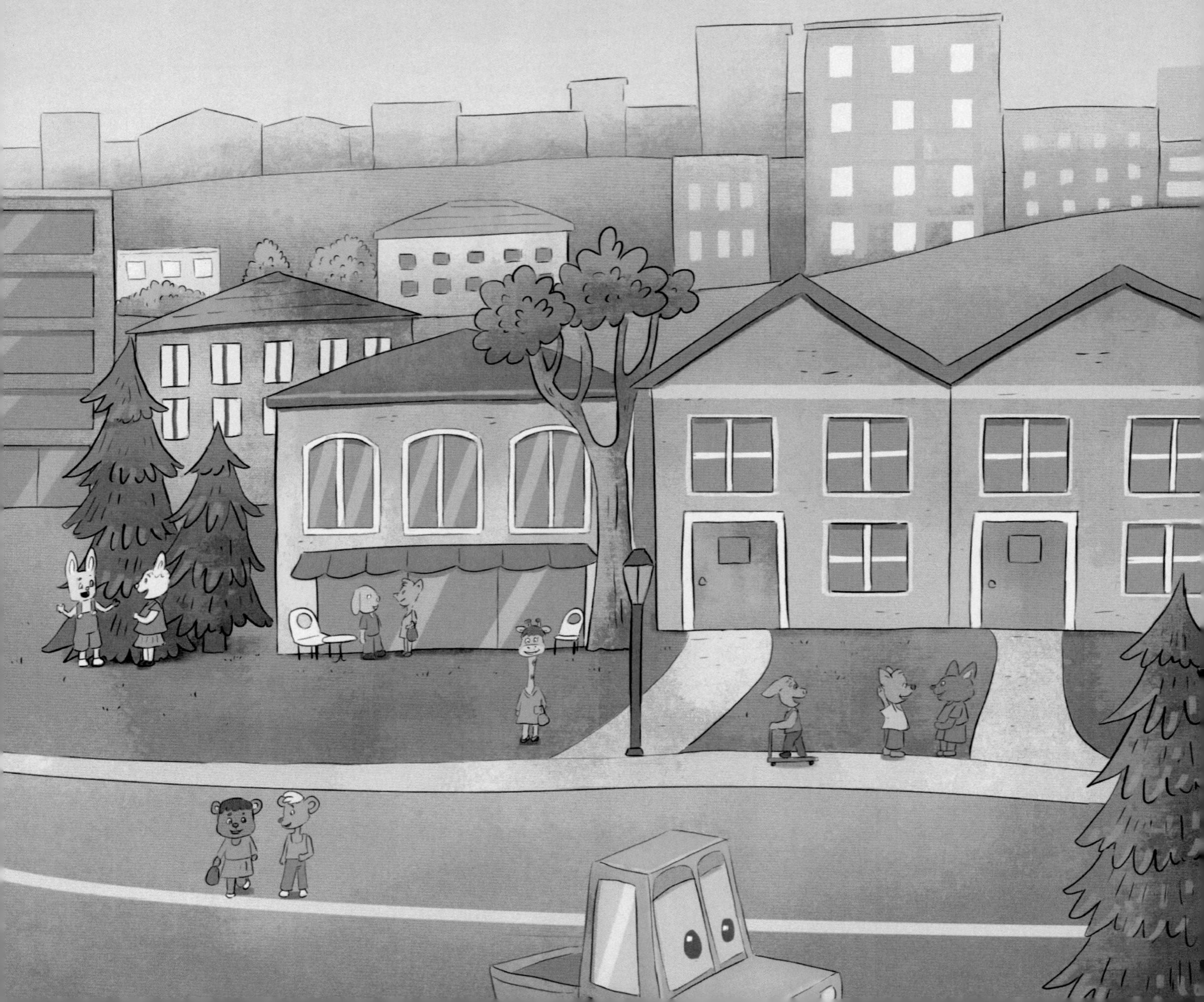

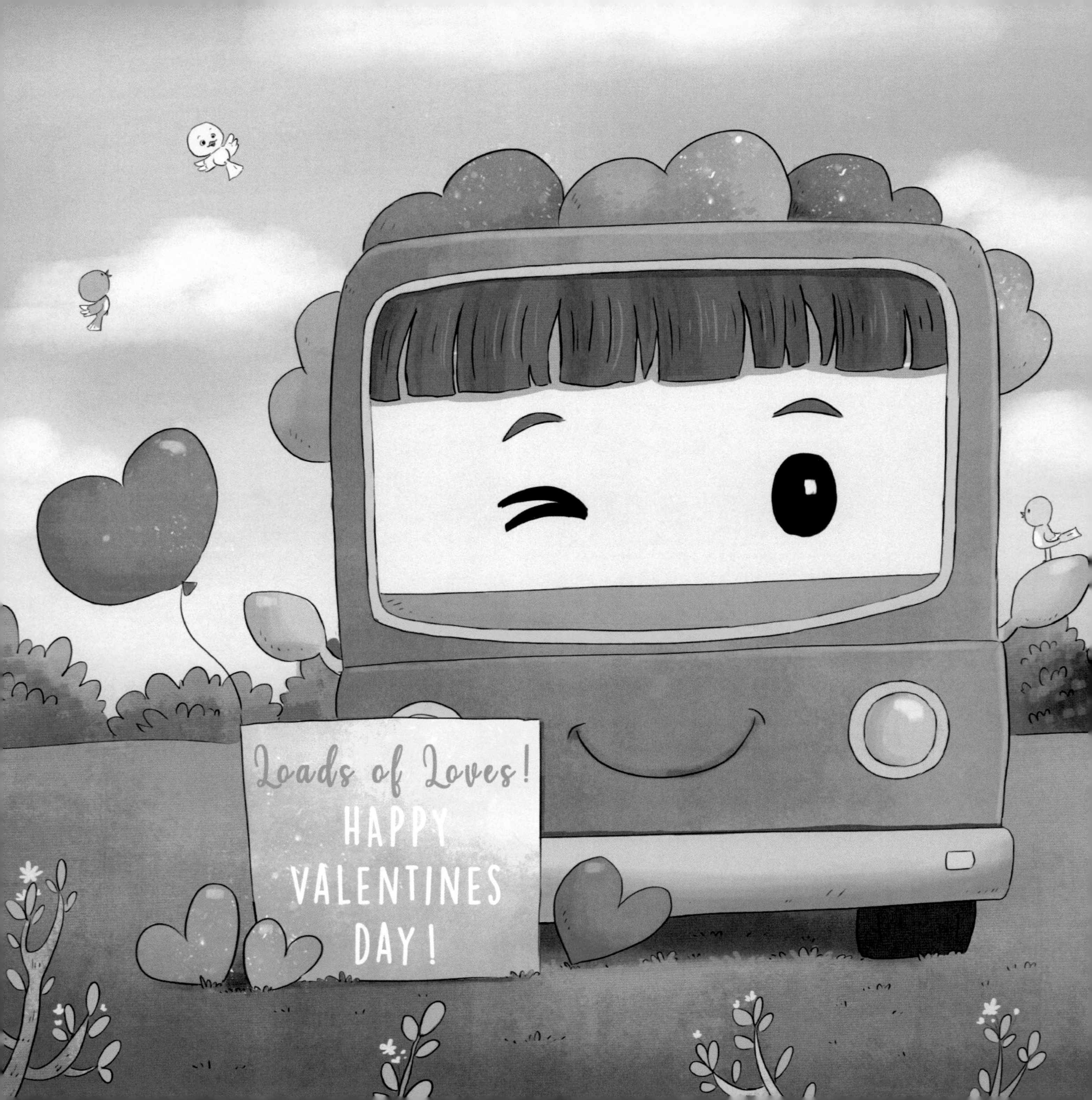
Loads of Loves!
HAPPY
VALENTINES
DAY!

That

special someone

is

YOU!

Happy Valentine's Day!

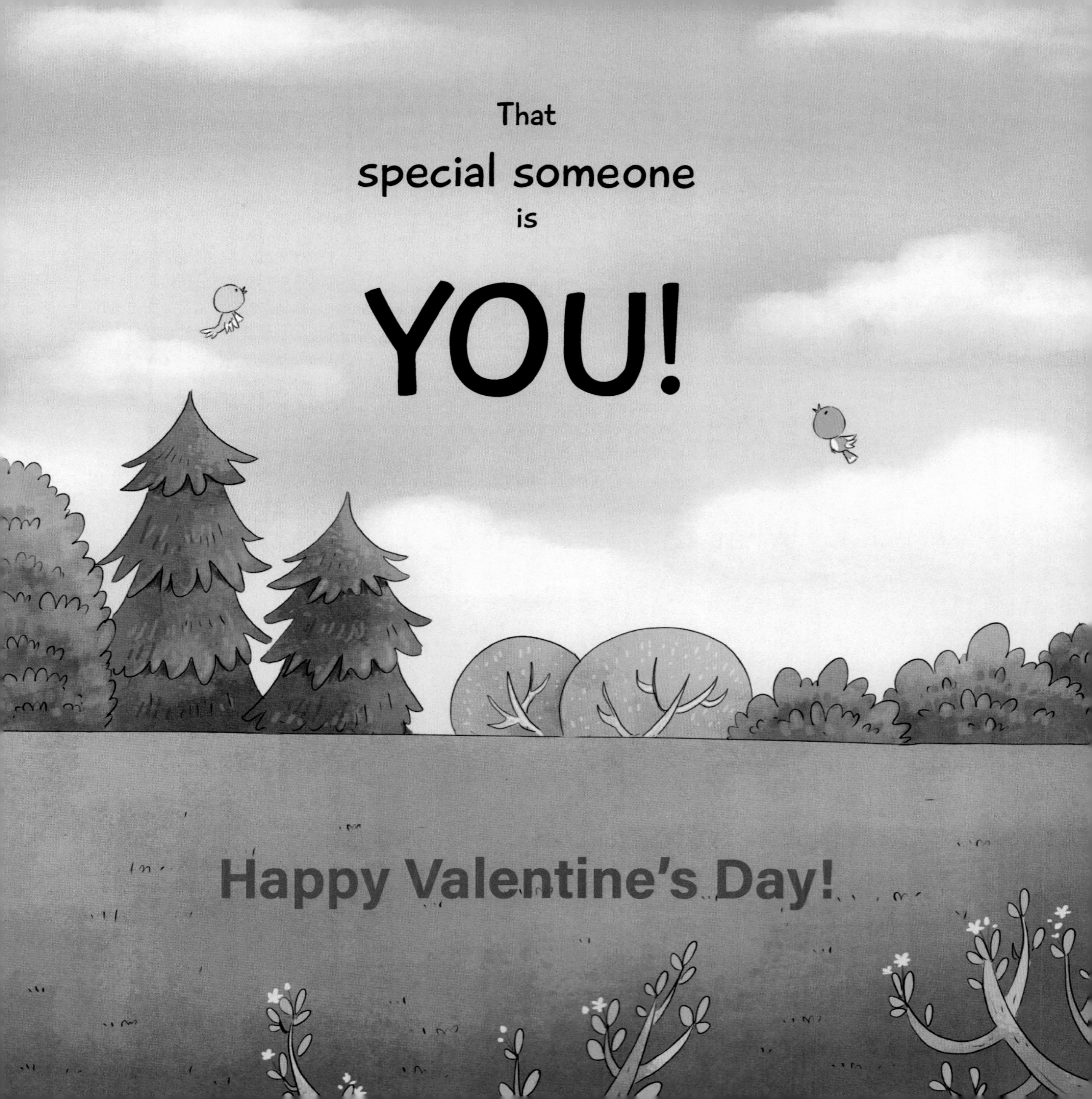

VALENTINE
QUIZ FOR KIDS

What color do you love?

What book do you love most?

What toy do you love the most?

What food do you love?

What do you love most about yourself?

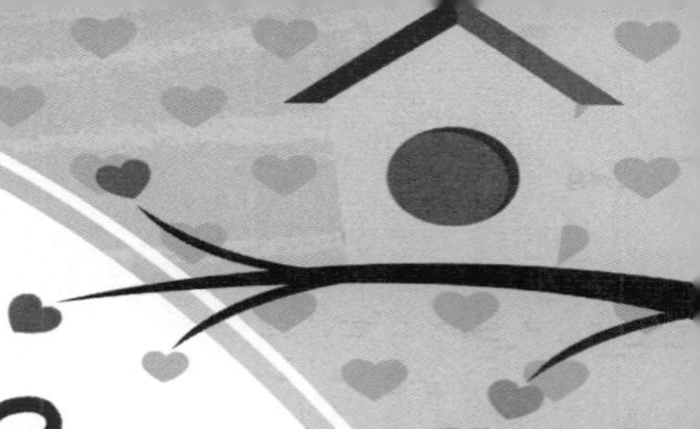

VALENTINE
Would You Rather?

Have a pet mermaid or meet a talking unicorn?

Eat broccoli or chicken flavored candy hearts?

Play a Valentine game or watch a Valentine movie?

Write a Valentine poem or sing a Valentine song?

Now make up your own "Would You Rather?"

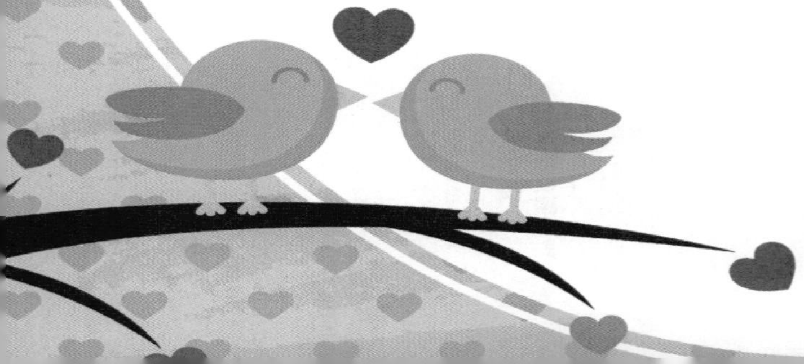

Made in the USA
Las Vegas, NV
27 January 2023

66371735R00019